SOUNDS FUN

A BOOK OF MUSICAL GAMES

TREVOR WISHART

Universal Edition

© Copyright 1975 by Schools Council Publications
© Copyright 1990 Reassigned to Universal Edition (London) Ltd., London
Printed by Halstan & Co. Ltd., Amersham, Bucks.
ISBN 900938 63 3
UE 26932 L

Introduction.....

WHY GAMES?

Group-games have been played from the most ancient times, and such games have often fulfilled a significant role in the life of the community e.g. in the religious ritual of the North American Indians. In more recent times, game-techniques have been developed for various kinds of group therapy, and have been used extensively by experimental theatre groups & groups working with children.

My first contact with group-games was with the theatre-games played by "Interplay" in Leeds. Since then I have developed a number of primarily MUSICAL games, some of which are presented in this book.

Games are a means of learning through group participation. Not only can we call upon the creative ability of each child in turn, but the leader of the group is seen to be participating in the game too, trying just as hard as everyone else to clap in the right place, remember the tune & so on. At the same time, the rules of the game impose a discipline on the group (each person must wait his turn) whilst retaining interest in everyone else's efforts. Thus games indirectly teach a mutual respect for the efforts of others, rather than a passive respect for authority.

Games are also a useful way to deal with disturbed or difficult children. In particular, especially demanding children can be given the role of group leader, director, actor, or conductor in the relevant games.

But, above all, Games are FUN; a way to learn something (perhaps without even noticing) while still enjoying yourself!

HOW TO LEAD A GAME SESSION.....

The games in this book are designed for from 10 to 40 people. Around 25 is probably an ideal number, but find out how many YOU can cope with.

It is most important to retain everyone's attention. If interest in a game is flagging badly, change to a completely different type of game. (CLAPPERS is a good game to gain everyone's attention). In DROPOUT games, make sure that all the people who drop out have plenty to do. Keep the pace up..... always think at least one game or variat ahead..... a short pause for thought can sometimes destroy the atmosphere of a session. Be ready to pick up cues from things that happen.

Let people think for themselves (& invent sounds, notations, conductions, ways of doing things). Encourage people, especially those who find it difficult. DON'T LEGISLATE.

Participate, and be seen to participate, in the games yourself. Let others start the games. Make it difficult for yourself (e.g. where it matters, put yourself last in the circle e.g. in ADDER). If you are stumped, admit it! Don't try to dominate.

Don't explain, DEMONSTRATE. If in doubt yourself, don't hesitate, begin, & sort out the rules as problems arise (the others will probably help you).

Some games are more difficult the further round the circle you sit (e.g. RIFF-RAFF, ADDER). So keep changing games from clockwise to anticlockwise & vice versa. If some people are always better than everyone else, make sure that they often get the most difficult plays (e.g. by being last in the circle).

Above all, plan your session carefully before you begin, and always have alternatives up your sleeve in case things fall flat. But be prepared to be flexible if the need arises.

THE DESIGN OF A SESSION.....

A session can be as long as you like, but you may find that enthusiasm flags beyond 45 minutes.

HELLO is a good game to start sessions, to introduce people to one another, & to introduce them to the circle-game format.

Move from familiar games to more difficult variants, or to unfamiliar games. DON'T try to progress too far all at once; there will always be another session.

Some games are concerned with Melody (ADDER, DIVIDER), some with rhythm (PLUG, SLAPDASH, RIFF-RAFF), some with counterpoint (RIFF-RAFF, TORTOISE), some with aural attentiveness (CLAPPERS, SONAR, PLUG etc.), some with aural memory (ADDER) and so on. You may (or may not) decide to focus on some particular aspect of music in a session & plan your games around this. However, don't be rigid.... if the session is flagging badly be prepared to switch to something completely different.

When planning a list of games always have alternative games or lists, or routes through the lists, in mind.

Also remember, if you don't enjoy your sessions, the group won't either. You should find it easy enough to judge the prevailing mood. At least always start with something which everyone enjoys.

DROPOUT games are a good way to move out of a session.

THE DESIGN OF A COURSE OF SESSIONS.....

Games may be used for any reason, from light relief from terribly serious matters, through being another approach to a general topic, to a means of progressive education in themselves. In the latter case, don't assume that you can start a new session where you left off the last. Always backtrack a little to refresh the group's memory, and always play a few old favourites.

THE LAYOUT OF THIS BOOK AND HOW TO USE IT.

Most of the games in this book are laid out on 2 pages as shown below. On the left hand page is an explanatory diagram, and the object of the game, after which a description of the game begins.

On the right hand page a number of variants on the original game are suggested. The number of possible variants is often unlimited & many others will probably occur to you. Try them out.

In the column on the right of the page a number of follow-up games are suggested. Where there is a choice of these follow-up games, your choice will depend on what aspect of music you are pursuing in the session.

Some follow-up games are linked to specific game-variants & these are placed opposite the description of those variants.

The list of follow-up games is not exclusive. In particular you may often want to switch to an entirely different type of

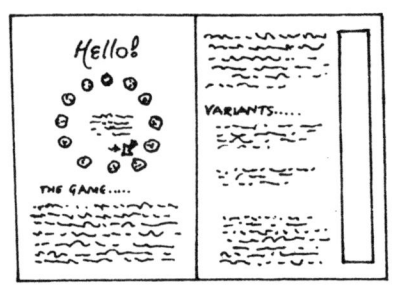

game during a session.

On page 34 the information in these columns is summarised in a flow-chart which you may use for planning sessions.

A number of suggestions for further activities is also included.

INDEX TO THE GAMES.....

page
- 8 .. HELLO
- 10 .. CLAPPERS
- 12 .. SONAR
- 14 .. ECHO
  DOUBLE ECHO
- 16 .. PLUG
  DOUBLE-PLUG
  DROPOUT PLUG
- 18 .. SLAPDASH
- 20 .. ADDER
- 21 .. DIVIDER
- 22 .. TORTOISE
  MULTIPLE TORTOISE
- 24 .. RIFF-RAFF
- 26 .. SOUNDTRACK
  PASS THE SOUND
- 28 .. CONDUCTOR
- 30 .. HARMONY-TAG
- 32 .. SUPERSOUND

- 33 .. DROPOUT activities

- 34 .. Session-Planner Flow-Chart
- 35 .. Further Suggestions

8.

Hello!

(.....this is an Inter-Action game)

an introductory game; a good way to start a session, to introduce people to one another, and to introduce the format of the circle-games.....
Everyone sits in a large circle.

etc.

THE GAME .....

The leader explains the game to the group as follows:—

Everyone will clap 3 times, together (led by the leader). Then everyone will leave a space (equivalent to 3 more claps). Then everyone claps 3 times again etc...... i.e:—

EVERYONE ♪♪♪ 7 7 7 ♪♪♪ 7 7 7 ♪ etc.

DO THIS.   Now, in the spaces, one person at a time will say his (her) name, starting with the leader & going round to his left (or right).

The game should then be quickly followed by two or more variants chosen from the list below, or of your own invention.

VARIANTS.....

1. Say what you had for breakfast/lunch

   Say what you did last night/in the holidays

   Say what you would prefer to be doing now etc.

2. Make a sound to express how you feel/how you felt last night/what you feel about the person on your right/what you feel about this game etc. → SUPERSOUND

3. Make a sound which uniquely sums up your personality (!) Use these sounds as the basis of "SONAR" → SONAR

4. Use the clapping framework, leaving plenty of spaces, to play the game "ADDER" → ADDER

5. Use the clapping framework to play the game "ECHO".... in this case the echo can be made by the next person to the left, or the person opposite. → ECHO

6. Use the format to tell a story bit by bit, each person adding his bit of the story as it progresses round the circle. The leader should sum up the whole story so far, from time to time (after every 3rd person say) so that no-one forgets it all. If you can't remember all of it, get the others to help you. Use the story for "SOUNDTRACK" → SOUNDTRACK

   .....Or move into another clapping-game → SLAPDASH / PLUG / CLAPPERS

10.

Clappers!

Send the clap around the circle as fast as possible

THE GAME.....

The leader explains that we are going to send a clap around the circle as fast as possible & indicates in which direction (e.g. to the left as in the diagram).

The leader (or anyone else) then makes the first clap and the person on his left (no.1, see diagram) must then clap as soon as he hears the first clap, and the person on his left (No.2) claps as soon as he hears no 1 clap; and person no 3. as soon as he hears no. 2, and so on around the circle, as fast as possible.

The leader may stop the game when the clap has completed its round of the circle back to him, or continue it by clapping as soon as he hears the person on his right clap.
  For a change, send the clap around the other way.

VARIANTS......

1. Send round 2 or more sounds, following each other around the circle. Begin with different sounds e.g. clap, stamp, hiss..... but later try 3 claps, & see how many get lost.
  For a change, send the sounds around the other way.

2. Send 2 sounds around in opposite directions e.g. clap clockwise, hiss anticlockwise,... Someone catches both sounds at once and must pass-on both.

3. Progress gradually from 3 to several sounds going round the circle in opposite directions. How many sounds do you loose?
  Send "Hello" to the left, & "Goodbye" to the right etc. etc. etc.
              (another pass-it-along game....)   → DIVIDER
                                                  → RIFF-RAFF
  (other games involving listening to several sounds) → TORTOISE
              (another pass-it-along game.....)   → PASS THE SOUND

Play any of these variants with EYES CLOSED → SONAR

Sonar!

A game for an even number of players, plus the leader who does not participate. You will require a large paper bag for each person (e.g. paper carrier-bags, large waste-disposal bags..... should be large enough to cover head & shoulders).

OBJECT of the GAME.....

To locate your partner by means of sound only.

THE GAME.....

Begin sitting in a circle; Firstly, number off 1,2,1,2,1,2 etc. around the circle, except for the leader who will not participate in the game. The No 1s become the partners of the No 2s on their left.

Next, everyone in the circle must choose his/her sound. The sounds should be as distinctive as possible. (NO WORDS or SYLLABLES!) Go round the circle, each person making his individual sound in turn. EVERYONE MUST REMEMBER HIS PARTNER'S SOUND.

Thirdly, everyone stands up & the leader hands each person a paper bag, instructing him to put it over his head so that he cannot see anything. At this point the leader describes the object of the game & explains that when partners have located each other they may remove their paper-bags & watch the others!

Next the leader leads each "blindfold" person in turn into some different part of the room & spins him around sufficiently to disorient him.

When everyone is thus scattered around the room, on a signal from the leader ("When I say 'SONAR ON'...") everyone begins making their own sound & attempting to find their partner. On finding their partner they remove their paper-bags & retire to watch everyone else!

ADDER
DOUBLE ECHO

VARIANTS.....

1. For a more difficult game, play as above, but make your sound only on colliding with someone else; at all other times remain silent.

2. For an amusing variant, let everyone try to find the person who was sitting on his left in the circle. On finding the person, they both drop out and stop making sounds. In this case many people are left searching for sounds which are no longer being made.

3. Keeping the same No 1 - No 2 partners, let No 1s remove their bags & invent a number of distinctive sounds to mean STOP, START, LEFT & RIGHT. No 2s memorise these sounds. Now let No 1s lead No 2s around the room using only these sounds, & AVOIDING ALL COLLISIONS.

Alternatively, space No 1s (o) & No 2s (•) around the walls of the room, with partners paired-off as shown. No 1s guide No 2s to them. Any colliding No. 2s are ELIMINATED.

HARMONY TAG
DOUBLE ECHO
see p33 for DROPOUT activities.

14.

Echo!

Try to echo your partner's sound

THE GAME.....

The leader notes how many people are in the circle. If there is an even number, say 20, he asks people to number off 1,2,3......9,10, 1,2,3......9,10. If there is an odd number he merely doesn't count himself in. In this way each person will be assigned a partner sitting opposite him & having the same number (see diagram).

The leader explains the object of the game & then the person on his left (No 1) makes a sound which his partner (the other No 1) must echo exactly. Then person No 2 makes a sound, and so on round the circle.

If desired, sounds may be repeated a fixed number of times to give the echoer more chance to hear them.

VARIANTS......

1. **DOUBLE ECHO....** in this case No 1 & 2 make a sound each, simultaneously. They must be sure to be simultaneous (they should watch each other). They may repeat the 2 sounds, together, a set number of times. Their partners (the other No 1 & 2) must echo the 2 sounds, not necessarily simultaneously ...... No 1 must echo No 1's sound, and No 2, No 2's sound.
   Then Nos 3 & 4 make a sound each, & so on.

2. Play TRIPLE ECHO, QUADRUPLE ECHO.... etc.

3. Play Echo or Double Echo as a DROPOUT game. If anyone fails to echo after a set number of repeats, then he or she must drop out of the circle & of the game.
   In this case, although you will start with fixed partners as before, when people drop out, partners will change. Just remember that the sounder passes round to the left, and the echoer also, regardless of who has dropped out..... e.g:-

1, 2, 3.... 8, 9 are SOUNDERS: 1', 2'... 8', 9' are corresponding echoers

Those who drop out should be assigned various DROPOUT activities to do, either singly, or in groups. See page 33 for suggestions.

16. Plug!

Plug-in the gaps in a rhythmic pattern

THE GAME.....

The leader demonstrates the object of the game (give a rhythm to the person on your right to clap, and you plug in the gaps yourself as he claps the pattern).

Next the leader chooses a suitable rhythmic pattern & begins to clap it out over & over again. e.g:—

|♩♩ 𝄾 ♩♩♩|♩♩ 𝄾 ♩♩♩| etc OR ||♪ 𝄾 ♪ 𝄾 𝄾|♪ 𝄾 ♪ 𝄾 𝄾| etc

Going round the circle to his left, each person must try to clap in the gaps in the pattern.

i.e. [rhythm notation] OR [rhythm notation]

♩ = leader ♪ = plugger

Each person has only one chance to fill in the gaps before the turn passes to the next person (on his left). If he fails, or plugs incorrectly, the game still carries on around the circle.

i.e. 1. [notation] | 2. [notation] | 3.fails [notation] | 4. [notation] | etc.

After one or two circuits, make the rhythm get faster & faster

For a change, play the other way around the circle.

VARIANTS.....

1. Choose longer, or more difficult, patterns to plug.

2. DOUBLE PLUG..... the leader claps one pattern and the person on his right SINGS a 2nd. The two rhythms should be in sync, and may be in the same or different metres

e.g. ||: [notation] :|| OR | [notation] | [notation] | [notation] |

Either send one plug to the left and one to the right (in which case someone may have to do a double plug), or (most difficult!) send them both to the left so that each person must plug both rhythms.

3. DROPOUT PLUG. Play as before, but this time, anyone who fails to plug or who plugs wrongly (or give people 3 chances) has to drop out of the circle & of the game. Assign DROPOUT activities to individuals or groups of people who drop out. See p.33 for some suggestions.

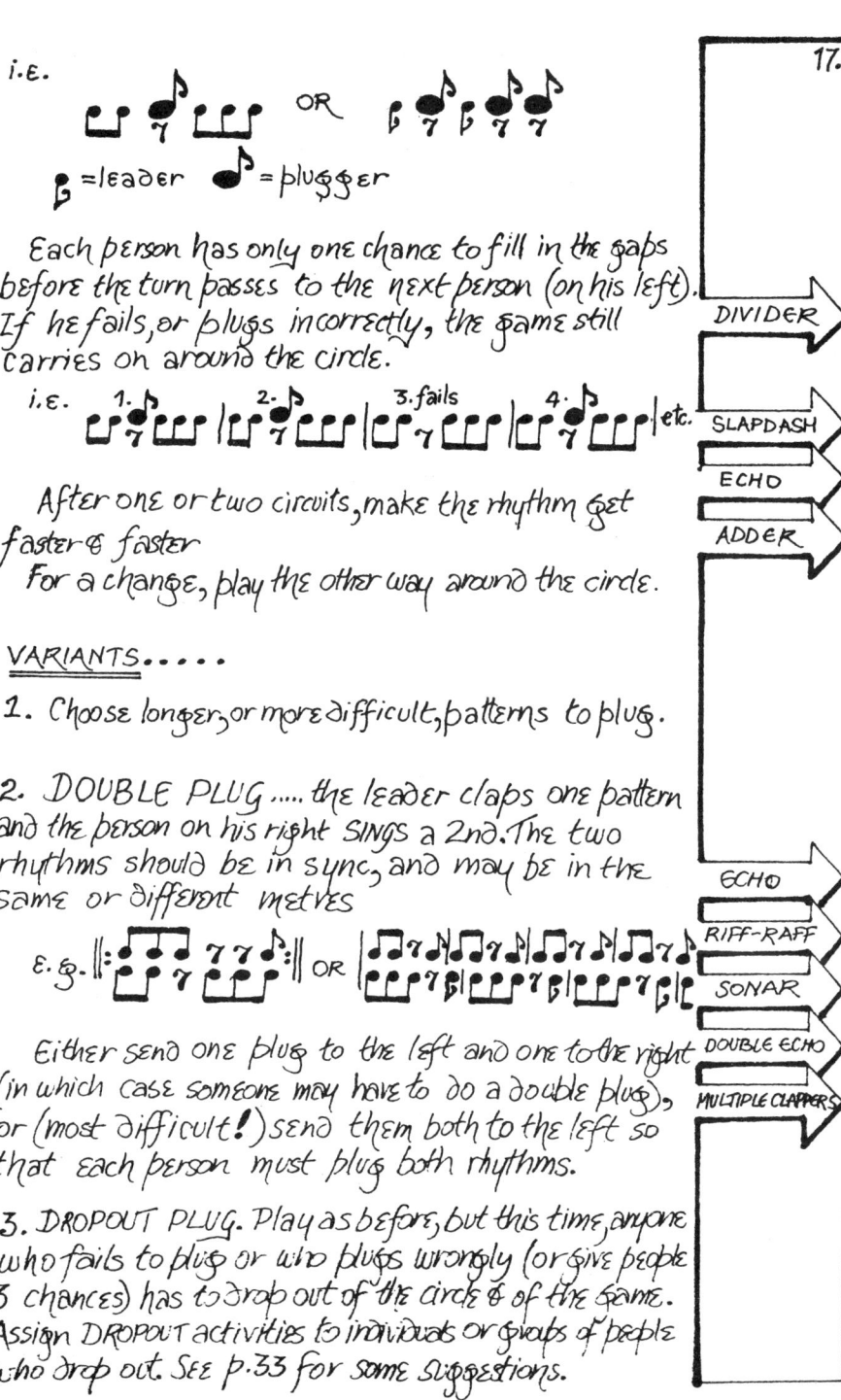

17.

DIVIDER

SLAPDASH

ECHO

ADDER

ECHO

RIFF-RAFF

SONAR

DOUBLE ECHO

MULTIPLE CLAPPERS

18.

Slapdash!

A game for an even number of people, forming 2 concentric circles. The people in the outer circle face those in the inner circle (& vice versa). People in each circle are spaced so that anyone may slap the hands of *Two* people in the opposing circle (see diagram).

OBJECT of the GAME......

As in the children's games (for 2 people), from which this is derived, to maintain a given rhythmic pattern at any speed!!

THE GAME.....

The leader first of all demonstrates a rhythmic pattern to the group, made up from any of the following:-

- ✶ ...Claps his own hands together
- ↓ ...Slaps his Left (Right) Knee with his Left (Right) Hand
- ᴿ↘ ...Slaps his Left (Right) Knee with his Right (Left) Hand

<u>BUT MOST IMPORTANT</u>:-
- ᴿ✶...Slaps his RH forward (into his (1st) opponent's RH)
- ᴸ✶...Slaps his LH forward (into his (2nd) opponent's LH)
- ⊠ .....or both at once

Everyone must memorise the pattern!

Everyone now forms the double circle & performs this pattern simultaneously. PROVIDED HE PERFORMS IT CORRECTLY anyone will find himself trying to slap his opponent's hand at the same time as his opponent is trying to slap his (producing a successful "CLAP"). If he makes a mistake, however, these 'crossclaps' will fail.

THE GAME GETS FASTER & FASTER.

→ CLAPPERS
→ PLUG
→ DIVIDER
→ RIFF-RAFF

<u>SOME PATTERNS</u> e.g.

invent & use any patterns you like, as simple or as complex as you need at any time....

[N.B. If you find this game difficult to understand, Try it out with just 4 people to begin with.]

19.

Adder!

Remember the tune and add a new phrase

THE GAME.....

The leader demonstrates the object of the game, & then begins by singing a 2 or 3 note phrase a set number of times (once, twice, four times).

e.g. ♪♪ ♪♪ ♪♪ ♪♪ (i.e. 4 times here)

Immediately after he has finished, the person on his left must repeat the phrase ADDING on a phrase of his own, and sing this whole thing the set number of times

i.e... e.g. ♪♪♪ ♪♪♪ ♪♪♪ ♪♪♪

Person No. 2 then immediately repeats the whole melody that no 1 sang, adding his own phrase e.g. ♪♪♪♪, the set number of times; & so on around the circle. If anyone forgets the tune (or gets it wrong) he begins again with a new phrase (Evolve a long melody and use it for composition or improvisation)

PLUG

DIVIDER

TORTOISE

RIFF-RAFF

CONDUCTOR

Divider!

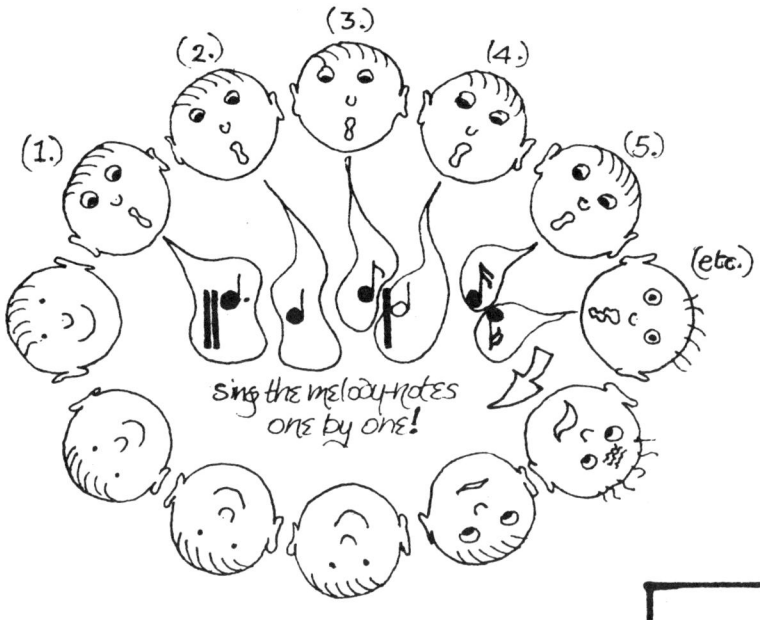

sing the melody-notes one by one!

PLUG →

MULTIPLE CLAPPERS →

ECHO →

THE GAME.....

The leader explains the object of the game & then invents a melody to use. He sings this a number of times, & then the whole group sings it a number of times until everyone knows it.

Then the group begins to sing it note by note, (No.1 singing the first note, No 2. the 2nd note, no.3 the 3rd & so on round the circle.) When the end of the melody is reached, the next person starts with the 1st note again.

Ideally the melody should have less or more notes than the number of people in the circle so that each person sings a different note of the melody when it is his/her turn to sing again.

Begin by aiming to sing just the pitches. Then try to get both pitch AND rhythm right! (Try sending the tune to the left and right simultaneously)

Tortoise!

Ride the tortoise, by fitting a counterpoint to a given tune

THE GAME.....

The group forms 2 roughly equal lines down 2 opposite sides of the room. The group-leader volunteers himself as Tortoise. The Tortoise has to think up a short tune which he sings over & over again. As he does so he crawls slowly on all fours from his line on one side of the room, to the other line. On reaching the other line he goes to the first person in that line who must, in the meantime, have thought of a tune which will fit in counterpoint with the Tortoise-tune. He mounts the tortoise & rides him back to the other line (slowly), singing the counterpoint to the tortoise's continuing tune.

On reaching the other line, the tortoise goes to the first person in that line who must have thought of a different counterpoint for the Tortoise-tune, and hence changes places with the first rider & rides the tortoise back across the room again.

The tortoise then proceeds to No.2 in the 1st line he visited, then No 2 in the 2nd line, & so on, and each time the same procedure occurs.

If, however, any person CANNOT think of a SUITABLE counterpoint then he/she becomes the NEW tortoise, and the old tortoise returns to his original place in one of the two lines. The new tortoise must invent a new tortoise-tune, and then the game proceeds as before, going to the next person who's turn it is.

When anyone has crossed the floor 4 (or any set number of) times as the Tortoise, he automatically ceases to be tortoise and the last person he arrived at becomes the new tortoise.

NB: Try to get the group to decide on what is PLUG and what is not a suitable counterpoint.

VARIANTS......

1. Keep the same tortoise-tune throughout (choose it carefully). All counterpoints must be DIFFERENT.
2. Try it with rhythmic counterpoints.
3. Use more & more difficult, or long, tortoise-tunes.

Multiple Tortoise...

The counterpointer LEADS the tortoise, instead of riding it, in this version. When they have both crossed the floor, the next person must add a tune to BOTH of theirs, & lead them both back across the floor RIFF-RAFF on all fours. The next person tries to add a further tune & leads all 3. Anyone who fails to think of a new tune becomes the NEW tortoise; the others return to their places.

24.

Riff-Raff!

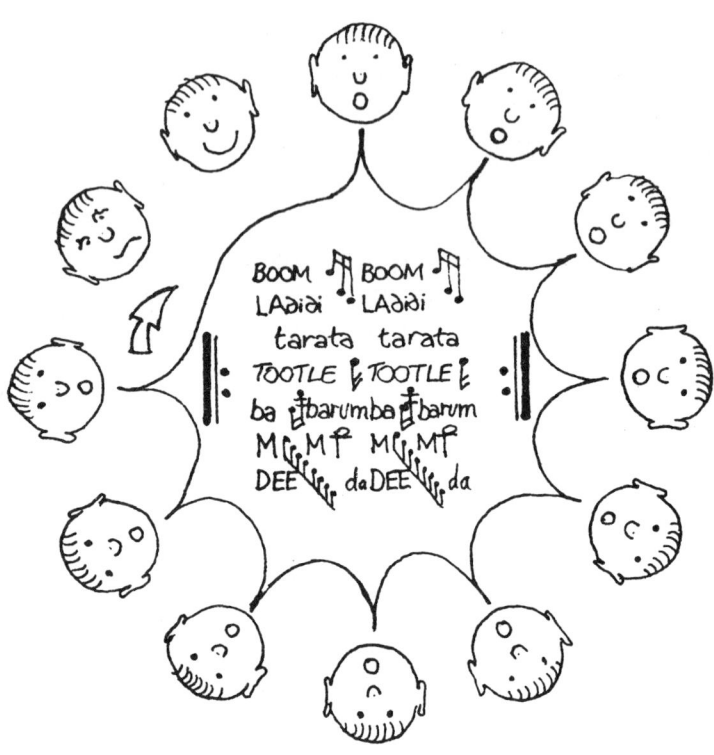

OBJECT of the GAME.....

To sing (or play) a harmonic riff.

THE GAME.....

The leader explains the object of the game (demonstrate!), and begins by singing (playing) a simple (bass) riff, over & over again.
The person on his left (say) then joins in with a suitable 2nd riff & they continue singing over & over again.....

e.g:— 2nd riff / Bass riff

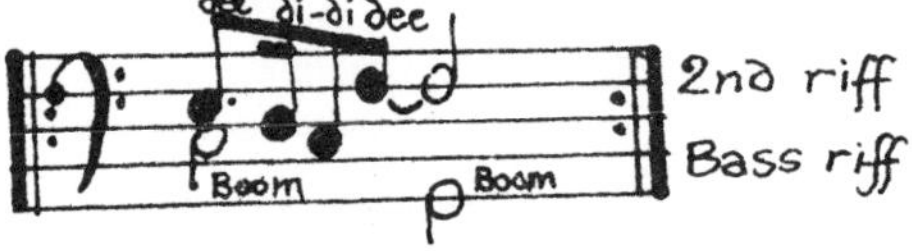

Then the next person to the left joins in with his new riff, & so on around the circle until everyone is singing.

NB: The lines need NOT be pitched, they could be vocal imitations of drums, cymbals, guitars etc, or real percussion.

HINT: If some people are much better than others at this game, put them as far round the circle as possible to make their choice of a new, yet suitable, riff more difficult.

When everyone has joined in, continue to sing for some time, then stop & choose a new bass-riff, or a new person to begin the round or both.

Also try moving to the riff. It helps to suggest new lines. Or get faster & faster until the riff falls apart. Or go on to add solos (see variants).

(You might use the riff as the sound-elements for...)

VARIANTS......

1. An easier version of this game can be played, using machine-noises instead of melodic-lines. Play it with the circle standing & linked arms-over-shoulders. When everyone has joined in begin to move the whole linked-circle round, in time with the machine. Get faster & faster.
Go on to act out a machine with sounds (see also "BREAD-SHOW MUSIC").

2. Play the original game using longer bass-riffs
E.g.:-

3. When everyone is singing the riff, improvise solos over it; each person is soloist in turn, going round the circle.

4. Improvise duets, trios etc. over the riff. Number off 1,2,1,2,1,2 or 1,2,3,1,2,3,1, etc to assign partners.

25.

→ DOUBLE-PLUG
→ HARMONY-TAG
→ SLAPDASH
→ CONDUCTOR

→ TORTOISE

26.

Soundtrack!

a music-theatre game

THE GAME.....

Object; to provide a soundtrack for a "silent movie"

(a) The leader assumes the role of "Director" and begins to tell a story. As he proceeds he points to anyone seated in the circle, who must immediately jump-up & act the part just mentioned, in the centre of the circle. This version of the game proceeds until everyone is acting a part.

(b) Begin again. This time number off round the circle I, II, I, II etc. as shown. The director will now point to the number Is only, to act in the story, while his No II partner (on the No I's left, say) makes the appropriate sounds to go with the No I's actions. (The "Director" should merely instruct No IIs to "make the sound to go with the action of your partner"; the rest is left to the imagination).

VARIANTS.....

1. Number off around the circle 1,2,3,1,2,3 etc, as shown. Now No 1s make up the story in turn while their No.2 acts it & their No.3 makes appropriate sounds. The story passes around the circle from storyteller to storyteller. (Clearly, every storyteller can only introduce his one character, his No.2, but this will be clear from the game-context i.e. when he has introduced his character, the next No 1. will take up the story).
   For a change, swap round the roles of 1s, 2s & 3s.

   (Also, use the sounds from this variant to play..........) CONDUCTOR

*2. Now there is NO STORY,....... number off around the circle I, II, I, II etc if you have not already done so. The No Is get up in turn to act whatever they like; and their No II partner makes sounds to go with the actions of his No I. (The leader may exemplify the game by being the 1st actor).
   For a change, swap round the roles of Is & IIs

3. Again there is NO STORY....... this game is similar to the game * above, but in this case the No IIs begin to make sounds before their number I partner gets up to act, and he must act out the sounds that his No II makes. Any No II may start & then it goes round to his left, one at a time, or superimposing more sounds & actors. For a change, swap round the roles of Is & IIs.

ALSO:—

Pass the Sound...

An invisible "thing" is passed around the circle — each person mimes a different object when he is passed the "thing" e.g. typewriter, baby etc. and then passes it to the next person. The person opposite must make appropriate sounds.

27.

CONDUCTOR

PASS THE SOUND

CONDUCTOR

SONAR

DOUBLE ECHO

SOUNDTRACK

SUPERSOUND

Conductor

THE GAME.....

First of all, each member of the group chooses a sound for himself/herself. (Go round the circle, each person making the sound he/she has chosen).

Next, anyone may be conductor (it will be unusual if their are no volunteers..... and after a short time with the game, most people will volunteer). The game may go on until everyone who wanted to be conductor has been conductor.

The conductor stands in the middle of the circle & by his hand movements causes different people to make, or stop making their sounds.

Rather than explain this, the leader should demonstrate this by being the first volunteer conductor.

In this way the conductor makes a musical piece.

At first it is often necessary for the leader to suggest the hand movements to be used, but after a time other group-members should begin to invent their own.

VARIANTS.....

1. As the game proceeds the conductor may invent new hand-signals for e.g. louder-softer, slower-faster, all together, soloist louder etc. If conductors do not begin to invent these themselves, group leader may suggest them and ask "how are you going to indicate faster?" e.g.-

2. After some experience with the game, the conductors may wish to use more complicated series of instructions, which can be done using symbols written on a board, which the conductor can point to e.g. if ✶ indicates "EVERYBODY LOUD" he may point to this symbol, & everyone makes their sounds loud.

In this way the group may gradually evolve its own notation system, and the conductors become composers.

3. At a still later stage, the conductors may ask for sounds to be changed, in order to make better pieces!!!

30.

Harmony-Tag!

A competition between 2 or more people to pick out a given chord (e.g. a triad) from a mass of sounds.

THE GAME......

Two or more people are chosen to be Harmony-Taggers. Then everyone else is assigned a note to sing or play (if the notes are to be sung, have a keyboard instrument in the room so that the singers can check that their pitches have not strayed). You should use at least all the notes of a diatonic scale, and eventually all 12 chromatic steps.

On a signal from the leader all the singers (players) begin to sing (play) their note continuously, and WALK around the room.

The leader next gives a chord to the harmony-taggers, such as a Triad, a Six-four, a minor 7th (but NB NOT a specifically pitched chord such as an E♭ triad, or a minor seventh on A etc). The harmony-taggers must now try to pick out 3 or 4 people, by tagging them, who are singing notes which will make up this chord.

The people who the tagger tags must stay where the tagger puts them & continue to sing (play) their note.

When the tagger finally feels he has the right chord, he shouts out "CHORD", & everyone, except those people he has captured, stops singing so that the taggers chord can be heard.

If the chord which is then heard is correct he wins & a new round begins with new harmony-taggers.

If the chord is not correct, he must start again & may not use any of the people that he first caught again. The other taggers continue as before.

VARIANTS.....

Ask the taggers to find more & more difficult chords (e.g. diminished 7ths, minor 9ths, and so on).

(move on to harmonically more difficult versions of.....)

31.

→ DOUBLE ECHO
→ SONAR

→ RIFF-RAFF
→ MULTIPLE TORTOISE
→ TORTOISE

Supersound!

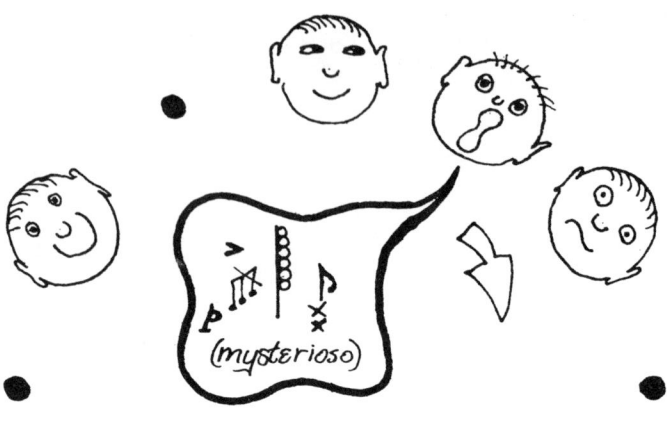

 make a sound which is completely original within the game...

THE GAME.....

The leader begins by explaining the object of the game. Then he asks the person on his left to begin. Each person in turn must make a sound which has not been made previously in this particular game. The game becomes more & more difficult as it proceeds!

You may place any restrictions you please upon the type of sounds to be used (e.g. vocal & body-sounds only, sounds made with objects only).

As the game proceeds you may gradually eliminate possibilities e.g. no combinations of previous sounds, no old sounds at new pitches, no words or syllables. The group as a whole may decide whether or not a sound is truly new. Anyone who fails to think of a new sound must drop out of the circle & of the game, and is assigned some DROPOUT activity :—

DROPOUT ACTIVITIES (a few suggestions)

FOR INDIVIDUALS OR GROUPS...

1. Invent an interesting 3-4 minute piece on ONE note

2. Go outside & listen to the sounds you hear. When you return, reproduce the sounds-outside, inside for us.

3. Invent a dramatic episode, but for the spoken dialogue, each person may use only his or her own name (to mean anything and to mean everything).

4. Think of ways to write down SUPERSOUNDS so that you can easily tell which one is which.

FOR GROUPS...

5. Take 4 short sentences. Try to think of a way to speak all 4 simultaneously so that each one can still be clearly heard. Try to think of more ways to achieve the same thing.

6. Imagine you have been to the Moon & discovered the music and dance of the moon-people (they have VERY strange music and dance). Play and dance it for us.

AND ESPECIALLY...

7. Invent your own new sound-game.

34.

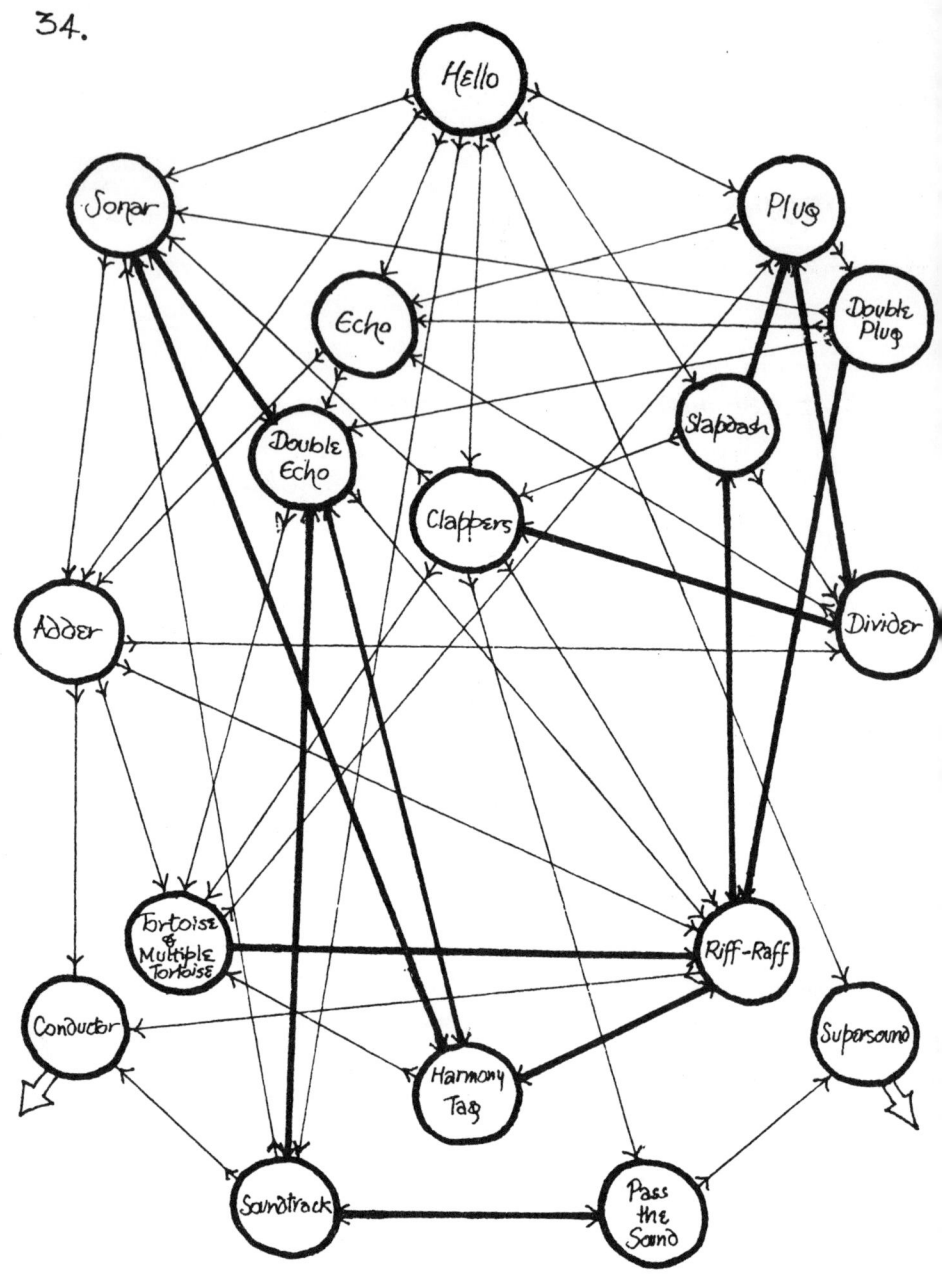

⟶ implies you can progress from the 1st game to the 2nd.
⟷ implies you can progress in either direction.

FURTHER SUGGESTIONS...

1. BREAD-SHOW MUSIC (Trevor Wishart, UE) extends the game Riff-Raff into a short music-theatre entertainment for children which can involve making simple props & costumes.

2. FOUND-OBJECTS MUSIC (Trevor Wishart, UE) is a natural extension of a game like "Supersound", and further game-procedures are discussed in this pamphlet.

3. A number of pieces of contemporary music may be regarded as open-ended games, and could be adapted for use with children. E.g.:–

    JOHN CAGE's various **"VARIATIONS"**
    TOM PHILLIP's "opera" **"IRMA"**
    & so forth

If you are interested in following-up the possibilities of using game-techniques in other spheres, (especially in drama-work) you should try to learn something about INTER-ACTION SESSION GAMES.